Foundation Stones

A Primer In
Carmelite History
&
Charism

Glenn Snow, O. Carm.

Carmelite Media

© CARMELITE MEDIA, 2025

First published in 2015.
Revised and Updated in 2025.

Carmelite Media
8501 Bailey Road
Darien, Illinois 60561

Phone: 1-630-971-0724
Email: publications@carmelnet.org
Website: carmelites.info/publications

Printed Book ISBN: 978-1-936742-37-0

Table of Contents

Foreword 5

Part I - There Is No Saint Carmel
History is Our Founder 7

Part II - A Carmelite History
It is Our Scars Which Define Us 17
The Conflicts of Carmelite History and Carmelite Life
   First Struggle: Prayer and Ministry
   Second Struggle: Challenger and Consoler
   Third Struggle: Protection and Expansion

Doctor, Doctor, Doctor!
The "Big Three" of Carmelite Saints 23
   Teresa of Avila: Revolution Through Transformation
   John of the Cross: Gold Refined by Fire
   Thérèse of Lisieux: A Thousand Drops of Water

Pressed Down, Shaken Together, and Filled to Overflowing
Two More Recent Carmelites You May Have Heard About 33
   Saint Titus Brandsma
   Saint Edith Stein

Part III - The Carmelite Charism
Three Pillars, Two Muses, One Allegiance 37
   Prayer, Community, Service
   Mary, Elijah
   One Allegiance
   The One Allegiance of the Carmelite Charism

Charism in Action: Nice Theory. What Does It Mean 49
   Living in God's Presence
   Listening to God's Voice
   Caring for God's People

Key Dates in the Order's History 53

Bibliography 55

Recommended Carmelite Websites 61

Foreword

"If you take from one source, it's plagiarism.
If you take from multiple sources, it's research."

Some guy who's probably in prison somewhere

This is a work of "research." With the exception of a couple of metaphors, a few alliterations, and an organizing device here and there, every idea in this primer is taken from someone else, someone who knows far more about the history and charism of the Carmelites than I do, even after 30-plus years of Carmelite life. Direct passages are cited, but not every sentence, for two reasons: 1) This primer is intended to be readable without jumping all over the place, or having the flow of every sentence interrupted; and 2) I claim almost nothing as my own invention. This is merely a convenient fly-over written in order to put into one small booklet some information that might be of interest to its readers. Instead, the bibliography in the back pages contains the names of the works which are referenced in the text.

Too many years of teaching and preaching have left me unable to give any account without including a personal story here, an attempt at humor there. I have not removed those from this little work, though I have tried to keep them from breaking the flow of the narrative.

This primer was written, specifically, to offer a very quick overview of Carmelite history and charism to the many people who work in various Carmelite schools, parishes, retreat centers, and other ministries. It began from a desire to give the faculty and staff at Carmel High School in Mundelein, Illinois, something in which the old-hands could recognize the Carmelites they have known... and the new-hands something in which they could glimpse the Carmelites they have not.

I have had the privilege of working in five different Carmelite high schools, one parish, and one retreat center, and in every place there have been colleagues who ask about the Carmelites, our spirituality, our history, and our life. This is written to satiate the appetite of some, and to whet the appetite of others. Fiat.

— Fr. Glenn Snow, O. Carm.
May 2015

Part I
There Is No Saint Carmel

History Is Our Founder

The Franciscans have St. Francis as their founder. The Dominicans have St. Dominic as theirs. The Jesuits have St. Ignatius. We have a bunch of people whose names we don't know. In fact, we don't even know how many of them there were, or when exactly they got started. We do have a location, however. And we have a general time period. So we have an historical context. That is important, because history created and shaped the Carmelites just as much as Francis or Dominic or Ignatius gave both genesis and form to their respective groups. **History is our founder.**

Because we have no single founder, our touchstone is Jesus Christ himself. That has given us a flexibility, and occasionally an ambiguity, which is different from many of the other orders and congregations. It might be argued that having Jesus Christ as our touchstone is no different from any Christian anywhere and that is correct. In fact, most Carmelites are quite comfortable being placed right in the middle of God's whole creation. The 1995 *Constitutions* of the Carmelite Order says that we live our lives seeking the face of the living God "through fraternity, and through service, in the midst of the people."

One of the hallmarks of Carmelite presence which is often remarked upon by the people among whom we minister is that there is little separation between us and everyone else.

"They're just regular people," is a refrain often heard wherever Carmelites live and serve. As Johan Bergström-Allen notes in his amazing book *Climbing the Mountain*, this life in the midst of the people is clearly expressed in the Carmelite emphasis on the humanity of Jesus. This doesn't mean our vision is limited to the historical details of the first-century figure known as Jesus of Nazareth. It means that we focus on the humanity of Jesus not as if it stood in contrast to his Divinity, but rather that we consider the humanity of Jesus to be the vehicle of his Divinity to the world. And because we are human, bound in this life to time and space and physicality, the vehicles of God's grace and God's presence are of utmost importance.

I can say without question that my mother loved me. That is more than a theory to me, it's my lived experience. The *vehicles* of my mother's love were many, varied, and enduring. She wrote me notes in my lunch sack. She hugged me and corrected me and welcomed me home. All of those, and a million other acts, were not just "signs" of a theoretical love, they were the vehicles, the means of delivery, of her very real love. Similarly, the humanity of Jesus was not separate from his Divinity. The humanity of Jesus was the vehicle of his Divinity to us physical, time-and-space-bound human beings. And so we focus on and emphasize the humanity of Jesus.

How does that look? How does that show up in our Carmeliteness? People will tell you that we tend to be down-to-earth, or even "earthy." We tend to recognize but not be obsessed with titles and hierarchical power structures. Our own leaders are elected for particular terms of office, and when those terms are over, they are just regular folks like the rest of us again. There are no life-long positions of authority in the Carmelites.

And so here we are, in the midst of God's people. Not in the midst of God's depraved and condemned people, but in the midst of God's redeemed people. In particular, by the resurrection of Jesus we've been swept up as well into the household of God. In the words of the Jesuit theologian Karl Rahner, God "has come to us Himself. He has transformed what we are and what despite everything we still tend to regard as the gloomy earthly residue of our spiritual nature: the flesh. Since [the Resurrection] mother earth has only borne children who are transformed." (Karl Rahner, *A Faith that Loves the Earth*). That means that in the humanity of Jesus our own humanity is redeemed. Since the Resurrection, there are no unreachable corners. Since the Resurrection, there are no unforgivable sins. **Since the Resurrection, there are no unsacramental moments.** In the simple words of the Carmelite, St. Thérèse of Lisieux, "Everything is Grace."

So as Carmelites who emphasize the humanity of Jesus, we can accept and even rejoice in our own humanity. And thereby we can accept and rejoice in everyone else's humanity as well, at least when we're at our best. That is why we're down-to- earth. That is why we're "earthy." It's in our spiritual DNA.

Part II
A Carmelite History

12 - *Foundation Stones*

If history is indeed our founder, then let us take a very brief look at the one who gave both birth and shape to us. The *Declaration of Independence*, one of the founding documents of the United States, was not fabricated out of thin air. It wove together the lived experience of the founders with the philosophical, cultural, and emotional intelligence of the ones who committed it to writing. The founding document of the Carmelites, the *Carmelite Rule*, came about in a similar manner. It reflected the lived experience of the founders, as well as the intellectual, cultural, and emotional intelligence of the one who put words to parchment.

In the late 12th and early 13th centuries, a scattering of hermits lived on Mount Carmel, occupying caves and huts in a shallow valley, the *Wadi ain es Siah*, which ran from the heights of the mountain ridge down to the sea-coast road in northern Palestine, near the modern-day city of Haifa, Israel. What brought them to this remote and primitive life is not recorded, but such a radical lifestyle is not usually embarked upon without some intense external and internal pressure. Largely hailing from Western Europe, some might have lived previously elsewhere in Palestine, but been driven from their refuge by military actions between Moslems and Crusaders.

Whether pilgrims, refugees, or even former Crusaders themselves, they lived near the year-round spring in this *wadi*, which was held to be the one-time home of the Old Testament prophet Elijah. The name "Carm-El" means "Garden of God." There was an alert, guarded, and perhaps even military color to their existence, reflected in the soldierly language of the Rule itself, which speaks of "the armor of God" and "the breastplate of justice." They had cause to draw themselves together, while still hermits, for common prayer and mutual support, and they formed themselves under an un-named leader known to us now only by the initial "B."

Somewhere around the year 1208, this group of men approached the Latin Patriarch of Jerusalem, Albert Avogadro, a papal diplomat of wide repute and influence, and asked him to draw up for them a *formula vitae*, a formula of life, which was both descriptive of the life they already lived, and proscriptive of the life they were to live from now on, bonded more closely to the Church by their official adoption of Albert's *formula*. One result of this transition was that it made the brothers (at that point, all men) accountable to each other in regard to their prayer and their relationships with one another. They had gone from being individual hermits, living in separate caves or huts, to being a community. Albert's *formula* became the first Carmelite Rule, and it was confirmed as legitimate by two popes. Most of them identified themselves by wearing the same simple un-dyed (gray-ish) garb consisting of tunic (body-length long-sleeved shirt), belt, scapular (broad flat cloth which rested on the shoulders and covered front and back down to the floor), and a large hood. They also had a woolen cloak with 7 broad vertical alternating dark and light stripes.

Their little chapel, dedicated to the Virgin Mary, became a popular landmark for other Christians in the local area, and they were known locally as the "Brothers of Our Lady on Mount Carmel." As their numbers grew, they began similar communities in the cities of Tyre and Acre, and even on the island of Cyprus. The truce between Crusaders and Moslems ended in 1240, and sporadically members of the Mount Carmel community began to travel back to Europe. Despite some hopeful military victories here and there, by 1291 the last of the Carmelites had either been slain or had left Palestine for safer lands.

In the meantime, those who had filtered out to other lands needed to adapt their middle-eastern customs, attire, meals, and practices to their new European environment. These changes were all incorporated into a new version of the *formula* which was approved by Pope Innocent IV in 1247, and which remains in large part today as the Carmelite Rule. Included in these changes were some adaptations which gradually changed the Carmelites into a lifestyle called the "mendicant friars." Mendicants were "beggars," that is, they retained no wealth from large land holdings or abbeys. Rather, they lived among "regular folks" and were dependent for their livelihood on the charity of the people they served. In the space of less than 100 years, the Carmelites had left their foundations in Palestine, had moved to a new continent and culture, and had gone from being solitary hermits, to monastic cenobites, to mendicant friars. They also ditched the gray outfits and adopted the brown habits they wear today. They bid special riddance to the striped cloak, which caused them to be ridiculed in Europe, and adopted a pure white cloak. In some places, the common nickname for the Carmelites is the Whitefriars, because of this cloak. It is used mostly on formal occasions nowadays.

If you want more history, there are several resources available. One of the easiest to read, and most entertaining, is a volume called *Desert Springs in the City,* by Fr. Leopold Glueckert, O. Carm. For now, however, I want to leave this simple account of our foundations and move to a non-chronological account of our history. We will still be examining Carmelite history, but no longer following it strictly chronologically. Instead, I want to examine our history by topic, not by sequence. Certain topics come up regularly in our history, and are a regular part of who we continue to be here and now. Because this primer is written primarily for people who work with us, I thought it would be helpful to know some of our more prominent "Carmelite characteristics" and where they came from.

One of the tensions, or the rhythms, which define us as Carmelites is visible in the transition we just touched on, from hermit to monastic to mendicant. From the earliest days on Mount Carmel, Carmelites have always moved between the worlds of quiet contemplation and service to others. That tension is with us to this day. There are Carmelites who live in the remote isolation of a hermit lifestyle, and those whose hours are spent almost entirely in charitable works of service. And even within us, individually, each of us struggles to find a livable balance, or rhythm, between the prayer of contemplation and the demands of charity.

The Carmelite Rule treats life as a conflict, a battle between the forces of good and evil both inside us and around us. I would like to use this metaphor as a means of examining some of the characteristics which any of you who work with us every day, could probably recognize as being part of our "Carmelite-ness."

16 - *Foundation Stones*

It Is Our Scars Which Define Us

The Conflicts of Carmelite History and Carmelite Life

The Carmelite Rule, our founding document, may be likened to a musical score. It is written in ink, brief, filled with symbols, and created to be performed rather than just read. Over the course of 800 years, it has been performed, lived out, by many tens of thousands in their individual lives, in small ensembles, and in large orchestras. The resulting music has taken many forms across eight centuries and myriad cultures. Each performance has its own background, tempo, and emphasis. Often times, the highlights of these performances have come in the struggles, the conflicts internal and external, which have been faced by those who seek to follow the *formula* of St. Albert. Several of these historical conflicts continue to be reflective of current struggles and rhythms in the many ways that Carmelites live out the Rule today. If you really get to know the individual Carmelites with whom you minister, you will find some or all of these struggles reflected in the way they, like every other Carmelite in history, live their lives.

The First Struggle: Prayer and Ministry

The Struggle in Carmelite History - Several of the reform movements in the Order's history have had, as a major component, differences in the way that prayer and ministry are valued and lived. Every member of the Order would agree that both prayer and ministry are crucial elements to the Carmelite, and indeed the Christian, life. Not everyone agrees, however, on the scope and the details of how that is lived out. Some would view the balance from a more global perspective, meaning that overall, we have some communities that are enclosed cloisters or hermitages, and we also have some more active communities. So therefore overall, we engage in both prayer and ministry. Others would put the focus on the individual Carmelite, meaning that every individual Carmelite is called to both contemplative prayer and to active ministry.

Realistically, the perspectives on prayer and ministry are a continuum, a spectrum with some leaning more heavily toward one side of the spectrum or the other. This is not new to the Order. The reform of Teresa of Avila, in the 16th century, was in large part a staking out of positions along this spectrum, and recognizing the value of these positions. The papal adjustments of the Rule in 1247 and again in 1432 were both attempts, in part, to clarify positions on this spectrum. The reforms at Mantua and Touraine were popular responses among the rank-and-file Carmelites to stake out their own positions on the relationship of prayer and ministry (as well as other issues).

The Struggle in Carmel Today - Today, we can still see the evidence of this ongoing struggle. There are cloisters and parishes, hermitages and high schools. On the individual level, it's easy to see how each Carmelite strives to create a workable rhythm of prayer and ministry in his or her own personal life and in the life of each community.

There are, since the 16th century, actually two Carmelite Orders known informally as "the Carmelites." The first is known, also informally, as "the O. Carm's" (pronounced as if it were an Irish surname) and the second is the O.C.D's, or "Discalced Carmelites." O. Carm's will occasionally acknowledge being addressed by the term "Calced Carmelites," though it makes us cringe. Really. Don't call us "Calced" unless you're looking for a shudder and an eye-roll. "Discalced" means "without shoes," because that group adopted sandals as part of their religious clothing.

These two branches came out of the reforms begun by Teresa of Avila, and originally differed about the place that Carmelites felt they should occupy on this prayer and ministry spectrum. The Discalced placed themselves more toward the contemplative prayer side of the spectrum, while the O. Carm's placed themselves more toward the ministry side. In reality, there is considerable overlap in how each Order lives and ministers, and the split is nowadays more of just an historical artifact than reflective of any major differences in values and lived tradition.

The Second Struggle: Challenger and Consoler

The Struggle in Carmelite History - The function of the Old Testament prophets was either to challenge or to console. The prophet Elijah, whose legacy is central to the Carmelite tradition, challenged the Israelites and their leadership when he saw how they had fallen from the faith of their ancestors. When he was staying at the home of the widow of Zarephath, her only son died, and in her grief she railed against Elijah and blamed him. His response was not one of challenge, but one of consolation. He felt her grief and prayed to God to restore the boy to life, which God did in answer to Elijah's prayers. Likewise, the young prophet Jeremiah challenged Israel in its arrogance, while Isaiah comforted Israel in its exile.

In our own Carmelite history, we have also lived out the melody and counter-melody of being challenger and consoler. John Soreth was the prior general, the head of the worldwide Carmelite Order, in the middle of the 15th century. John's challenges were directed almost entirely to the members and communities within the Carmelite Order itself. He promoted reform and corrected excesses in communities which he personally visited all over Europe. At the same time, his corrections were not heavy-handed or authoritarian. Instead, he tended to promote, support, and hold up as examples those Carmelite communities whose lifestyle and practices were more authentic, prayerful, and integral. In this way, he led his fellow Carmelites by drawing them from ahead by inspiration instead of driving them from behind by threat. John Soreth supported and promoted both the female branch of the Order and also welcomed and organized interested lay people into the Third Order branch. In the years after the French Revolution, when Carmel in Europe was almost wiped out, it was the Second and Third Orders, the nuns and the lay Carmelites, who continued to grow and keep the order alive in many places.

The Struggle in Carmel Today – Once again, we can continue to see this struggle as it is lived out in the lives of Carmelites today. Every one of us faces an internal task of balancing the act of challenging those we minister to (and sometimes ourselves), and comforting those who are mired in difficult circumstances. And again, it is not so much a choice of one over the other, but rather a rhythm of one feeding into and then drawing from the other. There are Carmelites who have spent much of their lives feeding the hungry, visiting those in hospitals and prisons, teaching and aiding those who are searching for spiritual guidance. There are also Carmelites who have spent their lives publicly and privately correcting, publicizing, and challenging the injustices which they witness in our world.

This, by the way, is the source of some of the most entertaining stories that Carmelites offer about one another. If you want to hear some good stories *from* Carmelites *about* other Carmelites, inquire about the ones who rock the boat and their interactions with the ones whose hands are on the tiller. The rhythm, and sometimes clash, between boat-rocker and boat-minder is evidence that the historical challenge between the roles of challenger and consoler are very much part of Carmelite life still today.

The Third Struggle: Protection and Expansion

The Struggle in Carmelite History – In 1841, there was only one Carmelite friar left in the once-thriving monastery of Straubing, Bavaria. In France, there were none. Portugal had no houses, and in Spain, the birthplace of Teresa of Avila and John of the Cross, a series of on-again-off-again government attacks had done massive damage both to the physical structures of churches and monasteries, but also to the organizational structure of the Carmelites themselves. The Spanish Carmelites, however, had absorbed the lesson of death and resurrection right down into their bones. Every time one or another persecution came upon them, they would hunker down and protect whatever elements of their tradition and structure that they could. When the persecution lifted, they would come walking out, brush themselves off, and go on living the Carmelite life in whatever new circumstances presented themselves.

It was not just the Spanish Carmelites who lived this death and resurrection, this protection and expansion motif. That one-man monastery in Bavaria grew man by man, and eventually sent out two Carmelites to the United States. These Carmelites named Cyril Knoll and Xavier Huber began an expansion of Carmel to North America, and founded what became the Province of the Most Pure Heart of Mary, a strong and thriving Carmelite presence even 150 years later.

The struggle between protecting what has already been gained and taking the risk to expand into new areas and new ventures, that struggle itself has been a part of our tradition since we peeked out of our caves in Palestine and looked around to see who else was out there.

The Struggle in Carmel Today – In Europe and in North America, the numerical ranks of Carmelites have dwindled. However, in Asia, Africa, and South America, the Order is flourishing like never before. In previous centuries, leaders like John Soreth, Nicholas Audet, Baptist Mantua and other reformers worked to call Carmelites to a simpler, more integrated living of their vows and of the Carmelite Rule. This often involved closing houses, moving people around, and encouraging them to focus on the basics of Carmelite life. The same seems to be happening in Europe and North America right now, as it happened in post-Napoleonic Europe, and previously after the Reformation. History was indeed our founder, and it appears that history itself is also our reformer, causing us to streamline and modify our commitments so that, like before, we can expand anew into a world which is still interested in and fascinated by Carmelite values, practices, and relationships.

This is reflected in the concerns you might hear from the Carmelites with whom you work and minister. Closing some ministries and starting new ones, handing over or handing back some institutions to the care of others…these are all difficult tasks which sometimes feel like a betrayal of tradition or an imprudent risk. But we have always struggled between staying put and moving on. Talk of the "good old days" is forever mixed with visions of hope for new ventures, new directions, new people, and new energy. These three struggles, among many others, have shaped both our history and our current life. The tensions and battles have produced scars, and their associated stories, which serve as testimony that Carmel is alive and well.

Doctor, Doctor, Doctor!

The "Big Three" of Carmelite Saints

As of this writing, there are 36 saints who are called "Doctors of the Roman Catholic Church." These are saints whose lives and writings have been determined to be of extraordinary value especially in teaching about specific areas of the faith. Three of these 36 are Carmelites: Teresa of Avila, John of the Cross, and Thérèse of Lisieux. It is interesting to note that the first two, Teresa of Avila and John of the Cross, are considered the founders of the OCD Carmelite branch. Although the OCD Order was not officially established until after their deaths (and therefore both Teresa and John remained OCARM's), the Discalced Order was comprised of the initial reform communities started by Teresa and John. Thérèse of Lisieux was also a Discalced Carmelite. In the United States, the National Shrine of St. Thérèse is operated by the OCARM Order.

Much of what the larger world knows about Carmelites centers around the life, the writings, and the devotion of many people to these three saints, all Doctors of the Church. There have been many people who have devoted their entire lives to studying and interpreting the lives and works of these three. The attempt, therefore, in this little primer to convey something of their contributions to Carmel and to the entire church will be necessarily broad and shallow. Some references to deeper resources are offered in the bibliography at the end of this primer. If there is a common theme to the lives of Teresa, John, and Thérèse, other than the general observation that all three were Carmelites, I can deduce only this: *Life is the art of letting go.* We draw closer to God, which is the entire point of this life, by letting go of all the things which hold us at a distance from God. The struggle is not to haul ourselves hand over hand, by our own power, as if we were rope climbing to the pinnacle of heaven. The struggle is instead to release, finger by finger, our death-grip on everything which keeps us from falling into the loving arms of God.

Teresa of Avila – Revolution through Transformation

Teresa was a revolutionary, make no mistake about it. Her vehicle, however, was neither force of arms nor force of law. She had no way of using that kind of force. The means by which she fomented revolution was through the resonance of her personal example. When an opera singer's voice shatters a crystal wine glass, or the booming of a radio shakes the rearview mirror, that is resonance in action. Something in one element, or person, emits an energy which at a distance touches similar elements in others, and sets them vibrating. The story of Teresa is the story of her resonance.

The time of Teresa was an era of reformation. The Protestant Reformation began, by common account, in 1517, and sent a shockwave of change throughout Europe. The Catholic Church responded with a collection of reforms of its own later termed the Counter-Reformation. One element of that was the Council of Trent, from 1545-1563. Reforming movements began in the Carmelites as well. Two prior-generals, Nicholas Audet and John Rossi, sought to translate the reforming spirit of the larger church into reforms within Carmel. Their position, as prior general, dictated that their reforms would be mostly "top-down," seeking to make change through traditional exercise of the power of authority. That is no doubt an unfair over-simplification, but every move by an authority, no matter how softly intended or subtly wrapped in cooperative overtures, carries with it the weight of office.

Teresa had no such weight. When she began her reform, she was just one more nun in a convent of about 180, all of whom had joined for various reasons and who lived within the convent under widely varying circumstances and luxuries. All of that didn't seem to make much of a difference to young Teresa until she had a personal spiritual crisis in 1554. She was reading the autobiographical *Confessions* of Saint Augustine, and had an experience of her own fallen nature, utterly in need of God's grace. She wrote: "How amazed I am when I think how hard my heart was despite all the help I had received from Him! It really frightens me to remember how little I could do by myself, and how I was so tied and bound that I could not resolve to give myself wholly to God" (*Autobiography*, Ch. 9). This is Teresa's focus in the "art of letting go." What she had felt "tied and bound to" were all the trappings of this life. In particular she strove to let go of the exterior trappings of wealth, status, and privilege. But she hardly stopped there. Not suddenly, but progressively, Teresa sought to let go of interior trappings as well. This meant letting go of distractions, letting go of the safety of superficiality, and ultimately letting go of anything that held her back from the all-encompassing embrace of God.

So what's the point? For what *purpose* did Teresa work so hard at letting go? For no lesser purpose than to be completely united with God. And she saw that as a journey, not an event. Her major writings, 1) her *Autobiography*, 2) *The Way of Perfection*, and 3) *The Interior Castle*, were all written about that journey, from the outside in, from the superficial connection with the world down deep to total union with God. The *Autobiography* is the opening story of her relationship with God and how God loved her and gave her grace after grace. *The Way of Perfection* was written as an introduction to a more spiritual life for the sisters who joined her various convents. It is probably the most approachable and easiest introduction into the writings and spirituality of Teresa. *The Interior Castle*, though purportedly written also just for her own nuns, is really an expansion of her concept of the mystical journey written to engage the whole of Christianity, i.e., not just her nuns, but anyone who wants to draw closer to God.

Teresa's spirituality, her writings, and her lifestyle drew many people to her, and made her a few enemies as well. She was indeed a revolutionary, but her revolution was one which was more about planting seeds than wielding a sickle. Hers was not a change dictated from a superior position of power or authority, but was a change inspired by people witnessing the transformation that she had attained in herself and in her communities. As more and more nuns were drawn to her various convents, she looked for Carmelite friars (men) who could support this new re-dedicated way of Carmelite life, and who could celebrate the Sacraments with these sisters. Foremost among the friars she found was a young Carmelite priest named John of the Cross. In John, she found someone who not only shared her values, but who experienced that mystical union which Teresa longed to impart to everyone. Even more, she found in John someone who had the ability to express, to put into words, the mystical experience of union with God which was beyond words. She found not only a poet, but an eventual Doctor of the Church, who became THE poet of the mystical life within the Catholic tradition.

John of the Cross – Gold Refined by Fire

St. John of the Cross was born Juan de Yepes y Álvarez, and was brought up living in hand-to-mouth poverty as his widowed mother moved her small family from city to city in search of some means for their survival. Notably, John's mother, Catalina, showed an active concern for others in need, and her generosity and faith was foundational in the formation of both her older son Francisco and her younger son Juan. John learned to read and write in a school for orphans and poor children, where he also learned the practical vocational skills of carpentry, tailoring, carving, and painting. As with many of us, an event during his childhood colored his interpretation of many later events in his life.

One day, when he was a young boy playing with some friends, he fell into a deep well outside of a hospital. It was so dark and deep that his friends thought he had drowned. John, however, floated to the top and stayed afloat, getting enough voice to yell to his friends up top to throw him a rope, whence he was brought up out of the well. He related at the time that the Blessed Mother had kept him safe and afloat, and John was devoted to Mary the rest of his life. It is not difficult to understand that the image of the dark well also stuck with John the rest of his life. After the orphanage school, John worked at a hospital, where he tenderly cared for the sick and gave free exercise to his profound compassion. The hospital paid for his education at a Jesuit college, and wanted him to remain as chaplain after the completion of his studies. But

John had discovered within himself a love for solitude and prayer.

At the age of 21, he entered the Carmelites, who recognized his passion and his intellect and sent him for further studies to the magnificent University at Salamanca, Spain, which was at the time one of the two or three finest universities in the world. But though he excelled at his studies, John's real interests were not in the world of academic theology. John was focused on the development of the spiritual person, the whole person, more than just intellect. After his ordination to priesthood, he returned to his home town to say his first Mass, and it was there that he met Teresa of Avila, 27 years older than John. The two became fast friends, and while John considered Teresa his mentor, she treated him as her equal. They very quickly recognized a common desire to bring the wide-ranging and lax practices of the Spanish Carmelites back to a more intense, and faithful, living out of the *Rule of Carmel.*

The reformed houses of Carmel, now both women's and men's communities, soon became an occasion of contention between those who wanted things to remain as they were, and those who wanted to bring the *Counter-Reformational* spirit to Carmel. In the battle which ensued, John was taken prisoner by the unreformed Carmelites, and imprisoned for nine months in a tiny monastery cell (really!). Flogged, starved, and subjected to intense cold and darkness by his "brother" Carmelites, John was thrust into a mystical crucible which he later identified as his "dark night." It is in a crucible that gold is refined by fire, and the gold that was John's spiritual brilliance was purified and refined during his imprisonment.

He escaped after nine months (perhaps with some help from a sympathetic friar, we don't know for sure), and was hidden away in a convent of reformed Carmelite nuns. When the divisions between reformed and old-school Carmelites became less openly aggressive, John was able to live more openly and without fear of further imprisonment. While he was prior of the monastery at Granada, the imagery which had both permeated and sustained him while he was imprisoned blossomed into poetry which is, to this day, taught as the highest example of poetry in the Spanish language.

John's writings are his most valuable bequest to history and to Catholic spirituality. They fall into two categories. First is the poetry itself, which flowed from the images he lived while imprisoned. Two of these poems, The *Spiritual Canticle*, and *The Living Flame of Love*, were written down during his six "safe years" in Granada. The second category of John's writings are his commentaries on the poetry itself. Altogether, John's most famous works include those two poems, as well as *The Ascent of Mount Carmel*, and *The Dark Night of the Soul*. Though he died at the age of 49, his last years were not a time of comfort and safety. Once again, his desire to adhere to a more strict and faithful interpretation of the Rule led him into conflict with other elements of the Order. He was sent to an isolated monastery and an attempt was even made to throw him out of the Order altogether. But John reveled in the solitude, and when he was dying from an infection in his leg, he asked forgiveness of the religious superior who was making his life difficult, because John "didn't want to cause trouble or inconvenience."

Therein lies the heart of John's spiritual and life stance of "letting go." For John of the Cross, letting go of his own indignation, letting go of his own pride, letting go of any desire for retribution, for recognition, and for status, was still only the visible facet of his intense, burning desire to let go of everything that would keep him from union with God.

The lives of Teresa and John were lived partially in vivid, visible, and political dramas that were seen and talked about even while they were alive. The life of Thérèse of Lisieux, however, was lived in a quiet corner of France where her life, and her death, went completely unnoticed by almost all except those who lived with her. It was only after her death that her fame and her influence spread around the world.

Thérèse of Lisieux – A Thousand Drops of Water

The fields of Normandy, in northern France, are not kept fertile by the raging torrents of a great river. There is no Nile, no Amazon, no Mississippi which waters the land and brings forth life. The fields of Normandy are fed by myriad drops of rain which fall on the landscape and provide life and growth, season after season, century after century. Such is also the story of little Thérèse Martin, the third Carmelite Doctor of the Church.

Thérèse was born in the town of Alençon, France in January of 1873. She died on September 30, 1897 at the age of only 24. If you approach the wing-shaped Vietnam Memorial, "The Wall", in Washington, DC, from the north at ground level, you won't be able to see it. From that perspective it rises only a few inches above the ground, and appears to be just a stone curb running east-to-west through the mown grass. But if you start at one end and walk towards the middle, it begins with only a few lines of names etched into the black granite. As you walk down the ramp towards the center however, moving lower and lower, you will find yourself dwarfed by an immense black wall, covered in the names of the American soldiers lost in that war. Finally, at the center, the wall towers 10 feet high above you, and you are swimming in names, overwhelmed by the profound depth of it all.

Viewed from the perspective of "the world," the life of Thérèse is just a tiny little curb running through a grassy field. She lived only 24 years and 9 months. She traveled only as a youngster, when she went to Rome with her family. She lived her entire life in northern France, and had no accomplishments which would make her visible to the outside world. A tiny little curb running through a grassy field. But walk with her down into the core of her interior life, and you will reach a depth of being, of spirituality, and of relationship with God unlike any the world has known. She was the youngest of five daughters, growing up in a comfortable home, and her family provided a tender, nurturing environment for their "little queen." At the age of four, Thérèse experienced the death of her mother from breast cancer, and Thérèse was thrown into a ten-year period of withdrawal, sensitivity, shyness, and melancholy. She was later enrolled in an all-girls boarding school, but it quickly became obvious that although she was academically outstanding, she simply did not know how to relate to her peers. Her sister Pauline moved into the Carmelite convent at Lisieux, and Thérèse again lost a mother-figure, causing her interior troubles to multiply. Thérèse was removed from the girls school at the age of 13, and was tutored privately instead. When two more sisters entered convents, her only remaining companion was her sister Céline. She had become, in her own words, unbearably touchy, and she prayed fervently to be relieved of this handicap.

Just before her 14th birthday, at Christmas in 1886, Thérèse had an experience on the stairwell of her home which she describes as her "Christmas conversion." In a single moment she relates that all her fears, her worries, her moodiness, and her self-centeredness was lifted from her, *not by her own power*, but as an utterly gratuitous gift from God. From that moment on, the final ten years of her life would be spent letting go of everything that separated her from the overwhelming love of God. Her life after that was not easy, but none of that mattered to her. She spent her life letting go of the need to be "big," to be "significant," and even to be "holy." The metaphor she used to describe herself was that she was no great beautiful rose... but only a tiny little wildflower visible to no one but God himself. Her supreme confidence in God's love led her to understand and embrace that God himself would accomplish through her whatever God wanted from her. All she had to do was let go and say "yes."

Thérèse entered the Carmelite convent at Lisieux at the age of 15 (having gone to Rome to ask the Pope himself for permission to enter at such a young age). She prayed, she swept floors, she did laundry and gardening, she washed dishes, she taught the newcomers. Her life in the convent was not one of great deeds and visible heroics. It was instead the living out of her core belief that God had not called her to be "successful," rather that God had called her to be faithful, and that's all that mattered.

In 1896, when she was 23, Thérèse coughed up blood, having contracted tuberculosis. There were no antibiotics and no treatments which made any difference in the course of this disease. She was also given no painkillers, not out of meanness, but merely as a matter of custom. It was in this period that she took to writing both her autobiography and an exposition of her spirituality, her "Little Way." Though she had begun writing earlier, it had been sporadic. Now several of her superiors, including her sister Pauline, directed her specifically to write them all down, which Thérèse dutifully did. During her struggle with tuberculosis and while writing her memoirs, Thérèse suffered intensely on a spiritual level as well. Spiritually desolate, feeling completely abandoned by God, her despair nearly overwhelmed her, and she felt such terror and darkness that she was unable to explain the depth of her suffering even to her sisters. But she continued to believe, because as she said, she wanted to believe. Her faith that God had carried her, imperfect and insignificant as she was, up the stairway, wrapped in his unwavering and loving embrace, made her confident that if God did it for her, then the all-loving God would do it for anyone else who sought it. Her "Little Way" consisted not of doing great things, but of doing little things with great love.

Thérèse died on September 30, 1897, and nobody noticed. Only the members of her convent had been with her, and outside the walls of Carmel in Lisieux, her death, like her life, had been unheralded. But her sisters gathered together her writings, some of which even they had not even read yet, and combined them under the title *The Story of a Soul*, which they sent out instead of the usual obituary to other Carmelite convents. These other nuns began lending *The Story of a Soul* to their friends and relatives, and by 1932, over 700,000 copies were circulating. A popular edition of the book also sold over two and a half million copies worldwide.

The life of Thérèse can be described as being nourished by a thousand drops of water. The love she showed on a daily basis, a thousand drops of water. The miracles reported after her death and attributed to her by people all over the world, a thousand drops of water. Her simplicity, self-sacrifice, trust in God, and poverty of spirit all combined to describe a giant in the spiritual life, who at first glance seems to be only a tiny curb running through a grassy field.

Pressed down, shaken together, and filled to overflowing

Two more recent Carmelites you may have heard about

Here are just a couple of Carmelites that you might have heard about, whose names have graced different buildings, rooms, or legends. The history of Carmel is filled with outstanding men and women whose lives, words, and actions have made them known in various periods of history. So I give you two more Carmelites whose stories reveal their own "letting-go" into the loving arms of God.

Saint Titus Brandsma

Titus Brandsma was a Dutch Carmelite who was martyred in the Nazi prison camp at Dachau. Titus was a professor of theology, steeped in Carmelite spirituality. He was also a journalist and spiritual advisor to the Catholic press in Holland. In 1942, he was arrested by the Nazis for openly and vocally taking a stand against the printing of Nazi propaganda in Catholic newspapers. Imprisoned in Holland and then in Germany, he was finally taken to the concentration camp at Dachau. There he secretly ministered to the other camp inmates and even to some of the guards and staff, without rancor or bitterness. He was executed by a lethal injection of acid on July 26, 1942. The nurse who injected him testified at his beatification and related how the conversation she'd had with him just before his death had remained with her, and had eventually brought about her conversion. A memoir written by another Carmelite at Dachau, Brother Raphael Tijhuis, presents an account of Dachau and of Titus' final days which is both fascinating and ghastly. You can find Brother Raphael's book *Nothing Can Stop God from Reaching Us* in the bibliography at the end of this primer.

Saint Edith Stein

Sister Teresa Benedicta of the Cross, (born Edith Stein), was also a tragic victim of the concentration camps during the Nazi regime. Edith was born to a devout Jewish family in Poland, and was an outstanding scholar of philosophy. She became philosopher Edmund Husserl's personal assistant, and in addition to her own considerable writings, she helped Husserl to organize and present his own work in a way that was more organized and understandable to the everyday reader. Her entire life to the age of thirty was spent in a deep struggle about her faith. In a single night, she read the autobiography of Teresa of Avila and declared "This is truth!" Shortly afterwards, she was baptized into the Catholic Church. She continued to teach until 1933, when Hitler closed all university positions to people of Jewish blood. At that juncture, she joined the OCD Carmelite community in the German city of Cologne. As the Nazis gained strength, her community was afraid that she would be in danger, and so transferred her to the Dutch Carmelite convent at Echt in 1938. Her safety at Echt was short-lived however, as the Nazis occupied the Netherlands in May of 1940.

On the day Titus Brandsma died, the Dutch bishops issued a strongly worded protest over the treatment of Jews by the Nazis. In retaliation, the Gestapo rounded up all Catholics of Jewish blood, and deported them to the death camps. Edith was put on a train bound for Auschwitz, and just two weeks after Titus's death, Edith and her sister Rosa were put to death in the gas chambers there. She was 50. Her philosophical work was marked by its profound connection with spirituality. Since her canonization in 1998, Edith has been proclaimed as one of the six patron saints of Europe.

The bibliography in the back pages gives additional references for these and other Carmelite saints and models.

Part III
The Carmelite Charism

What does "Carmelite Charism" mean, exactly? It's really just an answer to the question, What are you Carmelites all about, anyway? If you had to write down on paper what your entire life was "about", it would be a difficult if not impossible task. There's a similar difficulty in putting into words the charism of the Carmelites. In this section, I will try to distill down much of what we are "about" into some broad themes which both stretch back into our history as well as stretch across our current presence, our community lifestyles, and our mission in the world. To attempt that (and still keep things brief!) I shall stuff as much Carmelite charism as I can into the organizing theme:

Three Pillars, Two Muses, One Allegiance

The pillars are the three elements that are universally considered by Carmelites, past and present, to be the foundational required elements of living a Carmelite life. The muses are the two biblical figures, one Old Testament and one New Testament, whose spirit and legacy are the personal touchstones for authentic Carmelite life, prayer, and practice. The one allegiance comes from the Carmelite Rule itself, and is the destination point for everything Carmelite, both interior and exterior.

Three Pillars of the Carmelite Charism

Prayer: Each religious order in the Church, Carmelite, Dominican, Jesuit, etc., would include all three pillars in their own formulation of life, but for Carmelites, prayer is the one around which everything else clusters. For some religious groups and orders, prayer is a necessary activity which is engaged in earnestly in order to serve the world better, to be better ministers. Prayer is for them a means of making their ministry more effective and powerful.

For Carmelites however, prayer is not a means to a service-oriented end. For Carmelites, prayer is not a means to anything. It is, rather, an expression of our relationship with God. Prayer is first and foremost an experience of the presence of God. This is a prayer of listening, not of speaking. St. John of the Cross tells us that the surest form of prayer is to empty our minds of all thoughts and images (as much as possible... difficult for us human beings!), and simply to be in God's presence, to rest in God's presence. When Thérèse of Lisieux was asked what she says to God in her prayer, her response was "I don't say anything. I just love Him."

So by prayer, we do not mean reciting words or performing ritual actions. When Carmelites speak of prayer, we largely mean contemplative prayer. Contemplative prayer is our own participation in the "letting-go" which was central to the life of our founders, our saints, and our Savior. The letting-go of Teresa of Avila, (of pride, privilege, wealth, comfort, distractions), of John of the Cross (eschewing indignation, desire, status, recognition), and of Thérèse of Lisieux (letting go even of the illusion of self-sufficiency), are all accomplished in the practice of contemplative prayer. Contemplative prayer is not something we do, but rather something God accomplishes in us if we open ourselves to it.

Community: The second pillar is also written into our Rule and into our Carmelite DNA. The way God's kingdom will be built up on earth is through human beings living in communion with God and with each other. A sense of community, connection, with one another is therefore the primary way that all humanity is united. The word "connection" is not just an idea, a concept. It is a lived experience, practiced day in and day out, with real people. That means it's imperfect, and messy, and sometimes difficult. Community is also not a static structure, something that is contained in a certain format and follows all the same exact rules and sequences. Real community is organic, and fits the needs and styles of its constituents. When Teresa of Avila first joined the Carmelites, she joined a community of 180 nuns. Their practices were lax and their fervor inconsistent, and for 20 years, that didn't bother her much. As she matured, however, it became clear that such laxity was not how she envisioned the community she wanted. She needed something else, as did so many others who joined her way of life. In her reform, communities were to contain no more than 13 members, and they were to live their daily lives in such a way that every aspect of community existed to support contemplative prayer.

Both Carmelite history and current Carmelite practice are examples of the different ways that community serves our life. Even those who live in remote hermitages see themselves as connected to the rest of the Carmelite family, and to the Church itself. The call to live in God's presence in one's own room and to live in God's presence in community with other Carmelites is a challenge for which there is no simple checklist solution. It is a *mysterion*, a Greek word that denotes a way of acting, not just knowing. The various ways that Carmelites live in community reflect the reality that community is organic, a living thing that adapts itself to its era, its environment, and its members. Different forms of community, different experiments in living styles, have always been a part of our tradition, since we first came out of our caves and built common rooms in the *wadi*. Our struggles and tensions around community "in general", and within individual communities, are evidence that the same values and mysteries which first brought us together are still a part of our daily life and our Carmelite spirit.

Service: The third pillar of the Carmelite charism comes directly from the Scriptures. Jesus took the form of a slave (*Philippians 2:7-9*) and has called us to continue his ministry of service. HIS ministry of service. The ministry of service which Jesus carried out happened where he was, among the people who surrounded him. There were times when he instructed people quietly, as with the Samaritan woman at the well, or Nicodemus who came to him at night. There were times when he preached, healed and instructed amid throngs of people. There were times when he fed thousands and when he ate quietly with his friends. The service of Jesus was offered whenever and wherever he found himself.

Our service is a continuation of Jesus' service, and it too happens whenever and wherever we find ourselves. Some religious orders have high schools or missions or universities or food pantries or retreat centers or parishes or hermitages. In our history and in our present, we have all of those, whenever and wherever they have been needed. Carmelite service is not limited to one particular need or one particular ministry. In short, service is not about what we do, it's about who we are. It is not in competition with our contemplative prayer and our community, it flows from them. And any Carmelite will tell you (usually at length!) that our service feeds back into our contemplative prayer and our community life. They feed into each other and flow from each other, an organic whole.

What is important about our service is not the success it has in one or another venue. What is important is the love with which we do it. Thérèse of Lisieux wrote: "Our Lord does not look so much at the greatness of our actions, nor even at their difficulty, but at the love with which we do them." Tiny acts of service are available to us daily: a kind word, a smile to one who feels alone, a helping hand in a difficult task, a moment of instruction to someone who is lost. For Carmelites, service is not what we do. It is an expression of who we are. Those, then, are the three pillars of the Carmelite charism: prayer, community, and service. They undergird everything we are and everything we do. In order to understand and live these values, we look for examples in our lives and in our history. In particular, the Carmelites have two Biblical figures who form an inspirational foundation for living in the presence of God and bringing about God's Kingdom. Our three pillars are exemplified by our two muses.

Two Muses of the Carmelite Charism

In Greek myth, the muses were nine goddesses who served as sources of inspiration and guiding lights for the arts and sciences. In our Carmelite tradition, there are two Biblical figures who serve as our own muses, of sorts, although our muses are human beings and not goddesses. Both of them offer us guidance, inspiration, and occasionally correction. Since history is really the founder of the Carmelites, we have long looked upon these two as our flesh-and-blood foundational touch-stones.

Mary. The *Order of the Brothers of Our Lady of Mount Carmel*. That is the title, in English, of the Carmelites. Well, of the "O. Carm.'s". Well, really, the title of the male branch of that Order. History can be so limiting. But then again, history can be ennobling as well. One of the things that is common across all the Orders, branches, divisions, and flavors of Carmelites is the prominent place given to Mary, the mother of Jesus. That first group of hermits who became a community on Mount Carmel gathered for prayer in a chapel dedicated to "Our Lady of the Place"... and since "the place" was indeed Mount Carmel, the group became known as the Brothers of Our Lady of Mount Carmel. Though there are legends and stories about Mary and Joseph taking little boy Jesus on a picnic to Mount Carmel, there is exactly zero evidence (or likelihood) of that ever actually happening. There is an almost zero probability that Mary, through the entire time she was on earth, ever set foot anywhere near Mount Carmel.

It is arguable, however, that the real reason for the devotion to Mary of those first hermits was not due to some fanciful visit of the Holy Family to the Spring of Elijah, but rather to their acknowledgment of Mary as the first disciple of Jesus, and also as their protector against the rages of humanity and the ravages of time. It was *their* devotion and *their* presence which made her the Lady of the Place. And their medieval, feudal culture would have brought them naturally to devote themselves to the service of their "Lady" patroness.

As someone who works with Carmelites, one of the things you may occasionally hear among us is a reference to Mary not only as "our mother" but also as "our sister." It is fairly unique to Carmelites, and stems from the Order's title as the Brothers of Our Lady of Mount Carmel. What it really references is a fondness and affection for Mary that is positively familial. Not just in certain cultures or certain generations, but across the Carmelite world today and back through our history, Mary has always been seen from more than just a theological or historical perspective. For most Carmelites, Mary is a warm, welcoming, protective, supportive figure, and there are a few who would quietly harbor the conviction that the Carmelites are kind of Mary's personal obsession, and that she looks upon us with a fond and somewhat doting eye, like an older sister who watches out for her younger, sometimes mischievous brother.

There are many elements of the figure of Mary which are highlighted by different Carmelites in different circumstances. Sometimes the focus is on Mary as the first teacher of Jesus. She is also seen as his first follower. Mary is sometimes presented as the bearer of Christ, and we who are Christians also thereby become Christ-bearers to the world. The Carmelite martyr Titus Brandsma wrote: "We too must receive God in our hearts; we must carry God within our hearts, nourish him and allow him to grow in us in such a way that he will be born of us and live with us as God-with-us, Emmanuel."

Mary is also revered in our Carmelite tradition as a woman of prayer, of contemplation. She is also a woman who built first the Holy Family, and later built up the community of the disciples, as attested to by the words of Jesus on the cross: "Woman behold your son. Behold your mother." Her entire life, certainly, was a gift of service to others, and indeed to the whole world. Thus Mary in herself models for us the three pillars of the Carmelite charism: prayer, community, and service.

Mary is often portrayed in art as "Our Lady of Mount Carmel", dressed in a brown habit with white cloak and looking indeed very "Carmelite". She holds the Child Jesus in one arm, and from the other drapes a small piece of brown cloth, the scapular. This small scapular is derived from the scapular cloth worn by Carmelite religious originally to protect their habit while they were at work... in a sense, a kind of apron. It serves as a constant reminder that our spiritual journey is lived out in the everyday, working-world events of our daily life. The brown scapular today is a symbol of belonging, to one degree or another, to the Carmelite family. It is held as a sign of personal devotion to the Lady of the Place, to the Carmelite Order, and also is a recognition of Mary's love and protection of us as her children who were given to her at the foot of the cross.

There has been in Catholic history a tendency, at times, to "deify" Mary, to make her more than human. That has never been part of our Carmelite heritage. Our view of Mary as Mother of God is balanced by our experience of her as our sister, and even more, as the mother of us all by virtue of Jesus' words on the cross. In the words of what is effectively our Carmelite "theme song" (the *Flos Carmeli*), Mary herself is the flower of Carmel, and as Titus Brandsma wrote: "The devotion to Mary is one of the most delightful flowers in Carmel's garden."

Elijah. There is much to love, to appreciate, and to admire in the fiery Old Testament prophet Elijah. There is also much about Elijah that we recognize in ourselves. Along with Mary, Elijah stands as a muse for us, serving as our inspiration in many ways, but also as a prod and a corrective as well. The emblem of the Order, the Carmelite Shield, is surrounded by a ribbon which echoes the words of Elijah: *Zelo zelatus sum pro Domino Deo exercituum*. This is a Latin phrase which translates Elijah's answer to God's question,

"Elijah, what are you doing here?" From the mouth of his cave, Elijah responded "I am filled with a jealous zeal for God."

Elijah (sometimes known by the Greek version of his name, Elias), was a prophet who lived some 900 years before Christ, and had an active role in protesting the watered-down and heretical practices tolerated by the leadership of the northern kingdom of Israel. The traditional nation of the Hebrews had been divided into two kingdoms, Israel in the north and Judah in the south. Because Jerusalem, the Temple, and most of the machinery of the Jewish religion was in the southern kingdom of Judah, the king of the Northern nation of Israel wanted to solidify his power, and so he began to promote the building of temple altars and the appointment of non-traditional priests in the north. This Israelite king, Omri, also sealed a deal with the kingdom of Phoenicia by arranging the marriage of his son Ahab to the foreign king's daughter, Jezebel. When Omri passed away, Ahab became king of the north, and his wife Jezebel (who was also a priestess of the Canaanite god Baal) became queen. It was Jezebel who was the powerful one, however, and her influence over her husband Ahab and the entire northern kingdom was the occasion for Elijah's protest. Worship of Baal brought with it not only theological heresy, but an elitist and repressive authority which brought suffering to the common people of the northern kingdom. This was the milieu into which stepped the profound and history-changing prophet Elijah.

The stories about Elijah, mostly contained in the First Book of Kings, reveal a man who lived "on the edge." At times, he got up in Jezebel's face, and at times he ran away scared into the desert. When he first challenged King Ahab, Elijah declared that God would bring about a severe drought in the land as punishment for Ahab's unfaithfulness. When Ahab, goaded on by Jezebel, sought to silence Elijah, the prophet high-tailed it north out of the kingdom, and hid out in the home of a non-Israelite widow in the Phoenician town of Zarephath (in modern-day Lebanon). When the widow remarked that if she fed Elijah, it would exhaust the last of her food for herself and her son, Elijah declared that God would feed them all. Her flour and oil supply didn't run out while Elijah was living there. When the widow's son died, Elijah felt her anguish and desperation and prayed that God would bring him back. God answered Elijah's prayer, and the son came back to life.

After three years of drought, Elijah went back to King Ahab and announced that the punishment was over, not because they had repented but because God was being merciful to his people. Elijah and Ahab (with Jezebel prominently behind the throne) had a heated exchange, and Elijah challenged all the priests of Baal to a contest on Mount Carmel itself. Elijah wanted to remove the presence of Baal from the land of Israel, and to remove the influence of Baal from the Jewish people. Since Baal was the Canaanite god of the storm, (rain, thunder, lightning, and dew), Elijah challenged the prophets of Baal to build an altar on Mount Carmel and offer a sacrificed animal there, but to leave the sacrificial fire unlit. Elijah would build a similar altar and leave the fire unlit. Whichever God was real would light the fire. A day of dancing and incantations and shouting left the priests of Baal exhausted, and their sacrificial fire unlit. Elijah poked at them and made fun of them throughout, all within sight and earshot of the throngs who were watching this biblical Superbowl. When it came Elijah's turn, he not only placed the sacrifice on the altar, he ordered it drenched with jar after jar of water. Then he prayed aloud to the God of Israel, and lightning (or fire) descended from the sky and set the sacrifice ablaze so intensely that it also burned up even the other altar. The people seeing this rose up and slaughtered the priests of Baal. Elijah declared the drought at an end and rain came again to Israel.

When Jezebel heard of her priests being slaughtered, she sent out agents to have Elijah killed. Elijah once again high-tailed it out of town and went to Mount Horeb, where Moses had receive the Ten Commandments. Hiding in a cave, he heard the voice of God telling him to stand by the mouth of the cave, because God himself would be passing by. At the mouth of the cave, Elijah witnessed a gale-force wind, but knew that God was not in the wind. Then came an earthquake, but God was not in the earthquake. Then a fire raged past, but God was not in the fire. Finally, a small, gentle breeze passed by, and Elijah hid his face, because he knew that God was there, in the breeze that is like a whispered voice.

There is little wonder why the early Carmelites found such profound resonance in the story of Elijah. In a time of trouble and division, Elijah went against the grain and stood up to the infidelity of Israel and its rulers. These former crusaders and pilgrims also had gone against the grain when they gave up their former lives to live, like Elijah, in the caves of Mount Carmel. Chased from one land to another by unbelievers, the Carmelites, like Elijah, found refuge in quiet places far from their original homes. Again, like Elijah, they recognized that the voice of God comes more in a quiet whisper than in earthshaking drama. In Elijah, these early Carmelites found a real foundational spirit. Some of these medieval friars even developed mythical stories about being physically connected to Elijah through a series of hermits hiding out on Mount Carmel from the time of Elijah to their own time. Like the myths about Jesus and Mary picnicking on Mount Carmel, there's not a shred of historical fact to support such a myth, but the need for connections to the founding spirits of Mary and Elijah created simple, mythical stories which pointed to a less flamboyant, but nevertheless very real and fundamental connection between the spirit of these muses, and the spirit of living Carmelites.

In the life of Carmelites today, the spirit of Elijah and the spirit of Mary coexist in equal weight in the minds, hearts, and lifestyles of Carmel. Sometimes a focus is placed on Mary as the quiet, prayerful one, while Elijah is seen as the fiery extroverted one. But really a case can be made that Mary was just as "actively prophetic" and Elijah just as "quietly prayerful."

The two muses of the Carmelite charism, Mary and Elijah, have lent their stories and their spirit to the expanse of Carmelite history and the breadth of current Carmelite presence. Both appear at the most crucial moments of the Gospels, Elijah at the Transfiguration and Mary at the birth and death of Jesus. The **three pillars** of the Carmelite charism, prayer, community, and service, are lived out in the stories of the **two muses**, Mary and Elijah. All of them point us to the one allegiance which is at the heart of every Carmelite vocation, of whatever style, whatever culture, whatever era, and whatever emphasis. That one allegiance is to Jesus Christ, the genesis and destination of our life.

The One Allegiance of the Carmelite Charism

Allegiance is a term which has gotten mangled in our modern culture. Some have equated it with fascism, or with blind loyalty, and point out the folly and the terrible consequences in recent history of an unthinking, unreflective adherence to one human leader or another. Others have relegated it to the dusty bookshelves of history, and deem it an antique which has no relevance in a global society. But for Carmelites, allegiance to Jesus Christ is at the very core of our self-understanding and our self-actualization.

> Many and varied are the ways in which our saintly forefathers laid down how everyone, whatever his station or the kind of religious observance he has chosen, should live a life of allegiance to Jesus Christ—how, pure in heart and stout in conscience, he must be unswerving in the service of the Master.

Those words come from the *Rule of St. Albert*, the founding document of the Carmelite Order. They follow Albert's one-sentence introduction of himself and are his first statement of purpose and scope for the hermits.

These medieval men would have understood allegiance in the terms of their feudal culture, where vassals owed an obligation of fidelity to their liege (hence, al-liege-ance), who in turn would provide for them and protect them. Those are neither words nor circumstances which have the same meaning for us today. Throughout eight centuries of history, Carmelites have had to re-interpret and re-live that allegiance in ways which respected their own understanding and their own cultures.

One of the greatest leaders in the history of the Carmelites, Blessed John Soreth, wrote to his Carmelite brothers and sisters about how we are to re-interpret that ideal, about the process by which we can make it relevant and living in each generation. He said that we learn how to adapt it from Jesus himself.

> Let the love of Christ kindle your enthusiasm; let his knowledge be your teacher, and his constancy your strength. May your enthusiasm be fervent, balanced in judgment and invincible, and neither lukewarm nor lacking in discretion. Love the Lord your God with all the affection of which your heart is capable; love him with all the attentiveness and balance of judgment of your soul and reason; love him with such strength that you will not be afraid to die for love of him. May the Lord Jesus seem so sweet and tender to your affections that the sweet enticements of the world hold no attraction for you; may his sweetness conquer their sweetness.

This is the balance of head and heart, the rhythm of action and contemplation, and the harmony of giving and receiving which is called for from every Carmelite in every age in reinterpreting for themselves the word "allegiance."

How then do Carmelites of today, the ones alongside whom you minister, understand allegiance in a way that respects both their current circumstances and the history which created them? First, we remember that our allegiance is to the person of Jesus Christ. This serves as a corrective to any other attachments and attractions that may enter our lives. It is far too easy to become focused on status, material comfort, pleasure, reputation, autonomy, and a host of other qualities of life which may even be good in themselves, but when they become the central focus of our lives, move us to imbalance.

Throughout our history, the Carmelites have had to use our allegiance to Jesus Christ as a corrective to these imbalances. Barely fifty years from our founding, the prior general, Nicholas of France wrote a letter to his fellow Carmelites (The Fiery Arrow), excoriating them for the ways that they had become lax in the practices of the Order, and the ways that they had allowed the lures of this world to distract them from their allegiance to Jesus Christ, which they had learned and developed in the desert. In this passage, he critiques Carmelites who would see themselves as preachers, but who practice not what they preach.

> Where among you, tell me, are to be found preachers, well versed in the word of God, and fit to preach as it should be done? Some there are, indeed, presumptuous enough in their craving for vain glory to attempt it, and to trot out to the people such scraps as they have been able to cull from books, in an effort to teach others what they themselves know neither by study nor by experience. They prate away before the common folk, without understanding a word of their own rigmarole, as boldfaced as though all theology lay digested in the stomach of their memory, and any tale will serve their turn if it can be given a mystical twist and made to redound to their own glory. Then, when they have finished preaching, or rather tale telling, there they stand, ears all pricked up and itching to catch the slightest whisper of flattery. But not a vestige do they show of the endowments for which, in their appetite for vainglory, they long to be praised.

Nicholas was not a guy you'd like to invite over to a dinner of filet and a nice Cabernet, and he's no doubt at least a little biased towards the contemplation end of the spectrum. But his point is drawn from that allegiance to Jesus Christ which serves as a corrective influence on Carmelite life and practice. It is not about "us." Jesus Christ is the master. We are but servants, and we owe Him our allegiance.

The second way in which our allegiance to Jesus forms who we are and how we live comes in the realization that in the Carmelite tradition, Jesus is first and foremost *a person*. He is neither an abstract concept nor a theological invention. He was flesh and blood, a human being who walked the earth in real shoes (or sandals!). If we truly honor and serve Jesus in allegiance, then we must honor and serve the other real human beings with whom we share community and among whom we live and serve. Carmelites are therefore people-persons. It matters not whether we live in neighborhoods, cloisters, or in solitary hermitages, our allegiance to Jesus always calls us to reflect our concerns not inwardly towards ourselves, but outwardly towards humanity. Doing that well tends to make us less "stuffy" than some others, a characteristic which is often remarked upon by the people among whom we live and minister. Accepting and rejoicing in our own humanity, in allegiance to the real *person* of Jesus, moves us to accept and even rejoice in the humanity of others. It is our allegiance to Jesus that allows us to live and be in relationship with one another, even the ones who drive us crazy. In the end, the three pillars of prayer, community, and service, and the two muses of Mary and Elijah, all serve as reminders, supports, and models of our call to live in allegiance to Jesus Christ. That is the crux of the Carmelite charism. The last section of this primer will be a reflection on how our Carmelite charism is lived out in action.

Charism in Action

Nice Theory. What Does It Mean?

The Carmelite charism that has been squeezed and stuffed into this small printed space is all well and good, but what does it mean in action? What does it look like? I submit to you that the charism, as it is lived out by the actual Carmelites among whom you work, shows up in three general ways.

Living in God's Presence. The prophet Elijah said "The Lord God of Israel lives, in whose presence I stand." In the spirit of Elijah, Carmelites believe that God both exists and is actually present, and that we live in relationship with God. We are called to recognize, to cherish, and to nurture that relationship. We are also called to give witness to God's presence before others.

In our **prayer**, we strive to become more and more deeply aware of the presence of God. That is, in fact, the purpose of contemplative prayer, to simply "be with" God, with all our faculties, heart, mind, and soul immersed in the presence of God.

In our **community**, we strive to accept the humanity of those we live with. That always involves a simultaneous journey to accept the humanity that is ours also. We do this not out of condescension or some misplaced sense of *noblesse oblige*, but because since the birth of Jesus, humanity is God's way of being in the world.

And since the resurrection of Jesus, we humans are redeemed and "share in the Godhead of the Word" (St. Athanasius. *Letter to Epictetus*). And so we strive to accept and rejoice in the humanity that is collectively ours, precisely because it is the body of Christ, God's continued presence in the world.

In our **service**, Carmelites find many and various ways of helping others to make vacare Deo, "space for God." That means space in people's everyday lives, not just on Sundays or at certain moments. Experiencing and acknowledging the presence of God in liturgy, in quiet prayer, in joyful occasions with family and friends, and in difficult and trying times, these are all places where Carmelites in their ministries seek to help others to live in the presence of God. All of our ministries, visible and hidden, are geared toward promoting an awareness of the presence of God in all things and at all times.

Listening to God's Voice. God not only is present, but God speaks. As we learn from both Mary and Elijah, sometimes God speaks words of comfort, sometimes words of challenge. But always they are words of love. Whether those words feel sweet or difficult, Carmelites believe that God knows only how to speak words of love, because God speaks what God is.

These words come to us in every experience, every day. If we quiet ourselves long enough and deeply enough, we can hear the whisper of God's voice in every moment. St. Thérèse said, "*Tout es graçe,*" Everything is grace. Everything is gift. And the gift of God is God himself. The wonderful mountain-top feelings of exhilaration, these are the voice of God. The emptiness of feelings of abandonment is also the voice of God. The words of Scripture are singularly important as the voice of God, but must be translated, understood, and lived out in our own words and actions.

> All are to remain in their cells or near them, meditating day and night on the Law of the Lord and keeping vigil in prayer, unless they are occupied with other worthy activities. (*The Rule of St. Albert*)

God's voice speaks to us in our experiences of community and ministry, as well as our more obvious experiences of intentional prayer. Carmelites are called both to listen to God's voice in all things as well as to help others to do the same. This combines **prayer** and **service**, all lived within the context of **community**.

Caring for God's People. Mary visited and stayed with her cousin Elizabeth who was in need. Elijah risked his life and stood up for Naboth, who was murdered by King Ahab in order to steal Naboth's vineyard. Sometimes caring for God's people is public and visible. Sometimes it is quiet and hidden. Carmelites are not bound to one monastery, one location, or one kind of ministry. At the end of his life on earth, Elijah was taken up to heaven in a fiery chariot, but not before he bestowed his mantle upon his successor, whose name was Elisha. It is not in the charism of Carmelites to see themselves as indispensable for all time in whatever capacity they occupy. It is rather in the charism and the history of Carmel to hand on the mantle to others, who must re-interpret, re-imagine, and re-live that charism in new times and new circumstances, using whatever gifts God has given them.

In the end, the three pillars, the two muses, and the one allegiance of Carmel all point to God's lavish, affectionate, and tender love for humanity. Carm-El, the Garden of God, is overflowing with the gift and grace of God, in whose presence, at every moment, we stand.

Timeline of Key Dates in the Order's History

- 1890 - PCM Province Established

- 1876 - Only 50 Houses and 727 People in Order

- 1864 - Straubing, Germany to USA

- 1790 - End of Carmel in France until 20th century

- 1592 - Discalced Carmelites Become a Separate Order

- 1583 - Mary Magdalen de'Pazzi enters

- 1580 - Carmelite Foundation in Brazil (First in the Americas)

- 1542-1591 - Life of John of the Cross

- 1515-1582 - Life of Teresa of Avila

- 1452 - Papal Bull *Cum nulla* – Women and Third Order allowed to join Order

- 1432 - Mitigation of the Rule

- 1256 - Constitution

- 1247 - Mitigation of Rule

- 1214 - Albert Assassinated

- 1207 (cerca) - *Formula vitae*

Bibliography

General Works

Bergström-Allen, Johan (ed), *Climbing the Mountain: The Carmelite Journey***, 2014.**

This is the book to give you an understanding of Carmel in the world today! Bergström-Allen is a Third Order Carmelite (Lay Carmelite), which means he's not a priest, brother, (or sister!), but rather a lay person who has both immersed himself in, and bonded himself to, the Carmelite Order. He lives in the city of York, England. The book is 608 pages long, and is masterfully written, organized, and illustrated. It is written specifically with the Lay Carmelites in mind, and is the foundation of Lay Carmelite instruction and formation in the English language. There's almost no corner of Carmelite life that is not treated in this book. It's amazing.

Glueckert, Leopold. *Desert Springs in the City: a Concise History of the Carmelites.* **Darien, IL: Carmelite Media, 2012.**

Fr. Glueckert is a Carmelite (O. Carm.) in the PCM Province of the Order, and is a longtime teacher. While his resumé might label him a teacher and university professor, he describes himself (quite accurately) as a story-teller. This book takes the broad scope of Carmelite history, strips out the boring stuff, and presents the characters, the conflicts, and the core of our Carmelite history in a way that is positively a delight to read from beginning to end.

Welch, John. *Carmel Notes-- A Compendium of Carmelite Spirituality.* **Darien, IL: Carmelite Media, 2012.**

Content in *Carmel Notes* was originally prepared for retreats, days of recollection, and other programs based on the Carmelite tradition.

This work offers an accessible introduction to Carmelite spirituality. *Carmel Notes* presents Carmel's understanding of the human heart and its infinite desires. It proceeds to introduce three Carmelite Doctors of the Church and identifies fundamental themes in their spiritual teachings. Other major figures in the Carmelite tradition are then highlighted. Notes concludes with an introduction to the Rule of Carmel.

The Carmelite tradition encourages a listening heart, a contemplative attention to God's merciful presence. This book provides the reader with resources for an interior, spiritual life.

Works on Specific Topics

(in non-alphabetical order)

Batsis, Thomas M. *Carmelite Prayer and the Practice of Virtues.* **Darien, Illinois: Carmelite Media, 2025.**

The purpose of this book is to help believers come to a deeper understanding of what's involved in this journey to deepening one's faith experience. Rather than proposing a strict format of mental prayer, the author suggests readers identify a form of prayer evolving from one's everyday experience. He emphasizes the need to be flexible in prayer, if one is to discover that God seeks to be revealed within the context of each person's life. A section of the book includes a series of discussion and reflection questions linked to each chapter.

Tijhuis, Rafaël. *Nothing Can Stop God from Reaching Us: A Dachau Diary by a Survivor.* Roma, Italia: Edizioni Carmelitane, 2007.

Written as a memoir and a spiritual reflection on his experience following his arrest by the Nazis, this book recounts Brother Raphael's time in infamous Nazi concentration camps and prisons in Germany during World War II, including Dachau. It includes stories of his time with Saint Titus Brandsma, who was martyred there. Like the best of the recollections of that heinous period, it highlights not just the depravity of oppression, but also the deep spirituality and tender humanity of so many whose stories remain otherwise hidden to history.

Welch, John. *Seasons of the Heart: The Spiritual Dynamic of the Carmelite Life.* Darien, Illinois: Carmelite Media, 2008.

Written by Fr. John Welch, former provincial of the Carmelite PCM province, this book combines Jack's gentle personal style with a deep and profound familiarity with Carmelite spirituality. Reading this book is almost like having a conversation with Jack, imparting both an acceptance of our humanity and a reminder that our call is not to "stay put," but to move closer and closer to God. This small book weaves a modern pastoral understanding together with threads of the classic Carmelite spiritual masters into a flowing presentation of what the practice of the presence of God looks like today, and how it is accomplished in us by God.

Larkin, Ernest E. *Christian Meditation: Contemplative Prayer for Today.* Singapore: Medio Media, 2007.

Ernie Larkin, O. Carm., was a pioneer in contemplative Carmelite prayer. This was his last book, finished just before he passed away in 2006. This book is unique in that it does not begin with theoretical foundations either of a scriptural or theological bent. It begins with the story of Ernie's own prayer life, and the journey he engaged in while he lived his Carmelite vocation. Every page is filled with his own descriptions of different approaches to prayer and different moments in prayer. But he doesn't stop with descriptions. Ernie's broad and deep embrace of John, Teresa, and other classic teachers of prayer allows him to analyze and interlace their insights with his own experience, to the benefit of anyone interested in the practice of contemplation.

Boaga, Emanuele, [Joseph Chalmers, and Miceál O'Neill, translators]. *The Lady of the Place: Mary in the History and the Life of Carmel.* **Roma: Edizioni Carmelitane, 2001.**

I'm biased. I admit it readily. I included this book in this very brief bibliography because I always found it easier to understand a topic when it is presented in the context of its history. Boaga (translated by Fr. Joe Chalmers and Fr. Miceál O'Neill) presents a modern Carmelite interpretation of Mary by tracing the history of how Mary has been viewed by Carmelites over 800 years. This little volume is filled from beginning to end with passages and entire essays about Mary written by the most outstanding Carmelite names in our history. Reading through, which can't be done in one sitting or even ten, helps to clarify not just what we believe, but how we came to this belief by the road we have collectively traveled.

Healy, Kilian. *Prophet of Fire.* **Roma: Edizioni Carmelitane, 1990.**

Make no mistake, this is a book written specifically for Carmelites. Fr. Kilian Healy was the prior general of the Carmelite Order during Vatican II. He wrote this book, he said, because "we'd neglected this little titan far too long and left him in the hands of others." The term "little titan" could be applied just as readily to Kilian himself. The book examines each chapter in the life of Elijah, gives the text of the Biblical passage and a brief explanatory commentary on it. The heart of each chapter, however, is a dual examination of how Carmelites have treated this passage in the past, and also what it means for us today.

Welch, John, *Immersed in Mystery: Articles for an Interior Life.* **Darien, Illinois: Carmelite Media, 2025.**

The articles in *Immersed in Mystery* present transformations that result from living a spiritual life. The Paschal Mystery, the life, death, and resurrection of the Lord, emerges as a basic pattern necessary for a mature faith. An interior life is not a withdrawl from the world but an effort to have a true center in our life. It is an effort to have a spiritual life, a life guided by the Holy Spirit.

Millán Romeral, Fernando, *Truth in Love.* **Darien, Illinois: Carmelite Media, 2022.**

The English translation of Fr. Fernando Millán's well-documented research into the life and spirituality of St. Titus Brandsma and its relevance to many of today's situations. As a vice-postulator for the cause for canonization of Fr. Titus and former prior general of the Carmelite Order, Fr. Fernando is extremely knowledgeable about the Fr. Titus' spirituality and draws out connections not found in other works on Brandsma.

This volume in English has been amplified with recent information uncovered by Fr. Fernando which is not in previous translations. Written in a very familiar storytelling style, the reader will find the rich spirituality of this Carmelite saint very accessible.

RECOMMENDED CARMELITE WEBSITES

For more information about the Carmelites today, our spirituality and our ministries worldwide, visit:
The Carmelite Order: ocarm.org

The Most Pure Heart of Mary Province: carmelites.net

Center for Carmelite Studies at Catholic University of America:
carmelites.info/CenterForCarmeliteStudies

Carmelite Institute of North America:
carmeliteinstitute.net

Carmelite Media Publications Bookstore:
publications.carmelitemedia.org

Edizioni Carmelitane Bookstore:
edizionicarmelitane.org

For a listing of Carmelite provinces worldwide, visit:
carmelites.info/provinces

For a listing of Monasteries of Carmelite nuns, visit:
carmelites.info/nuns

For a listing of Carmelite Hermitages, please visit:
carmelites.info/hermits

For a listing of sites about Lay Carmelites:
carmelites.info/lay carmel

For a listing of Affiliated Congregations and Institutes:
carmelites.info/congregations

For our work with the United Nations, visit:
carmelitengo.org

For more information about publications, visit:
carmelites.info/publications

www.ingramcontent.com/pod-product-compliance
Lightning Source LLC
Chambersburg PA
CBHW041928040426
42444CB00018B/3463